This **book** belongs to

and

Teevra

TO OUR PARENTS

Kumar, Mridula   Rohit, kalindi

© 2017 Little Ustaads Arts Private Limited
This edition published 2018

Published in collaboration with Bloomsbury India

ISBN 978-09-99403-30-3
Printed and bound at EIH Ltd. Gurugram, Haryana

www.littleustaads.com
www.bloomsbury.com

NAMASTE JAIPUR

WRITTEN BY **Rachana Chandaria-Mamania** and **Kavita Bafana**

ILLUSTRATED BY **Sandhya Prabhat**

Let's travel to the Great Thar Desert on a bumpy camel ride.

We are off to see the pink city of Jaipur, Rajasthan's pride.

We squint our eyes in the blazing sun and watch the endless, rolling sand.

Remembering the maharajas who once ruled this rich and ancient land.

We can't wait to explore this magical city where everything is pink.

Hoping the ranis and rajas will welcome us with a rose sherbat drink.

We knock on the door of the City Palace hoping to meet the King.

The beautiful Peacock Gates open and Teevra runs to the queen's wing.

I catch Teevra and we walk to Hawa Mahal, where the air is cool.
Princesses hide behind jharokhas and watch children go to school.

"Namaste Bhaiya, can you take us to where the Jal Mahal floats?"
To cross Lake Man Sagar, we step into the wooden boats.

The Palace has a large courtyard, we decide to run and play.
Teevra starts licking the sweet lassi, left in a pot of clay.

At the foot of the Aravalli Hills is Kanak Vrindavan Gardens, a perfect picnic spo

Nani packed dal bati churma, a Rajasthani treat that's tasty and hot.

Peacocks flutter their blue feathers while water fountains cool the air.

In this paradise, stands krishna a with his magical flute and curly hair.

Ten large grey elephants stand in a line
Ready to show us where kings and queens dine.
We climb onto our elephant's strong back.
He sways and carries us up the stone track.

 Many Rajput families lived at the mighty Amer Fort.
A palace that protected the Kings and has a mirror court.

 Look! I am here. Look! I am there. I see myself everywhere.

But the polo match is starting soon, let's hurry over there.

Polo is a popular sport, where everyone cheers for their team.
We love to see the horses gallop past us as we jump and scream.

Why do stars twinkle? How far is the moon?
Let's explore Jantar Mantar all afternoon.

I push my brother aside to see a shooting star.
Everything seems so near, even though it's far.

"Aam! Aam!" shouts the mango seller pushing his cart through the streets.
The mangoes are piled up high, they smell so delicious and sweet.

In Tripolia Bazaar squiggly orange lines sizzle in a pan.
We eat ghevar and lick our sticky fingers as fast as we can.

We take a break, swing on a jhula and watch birds fly back to their nests.

The loud dholak beats, the puppet show starts, we are invited as guests.

Stiff wooden dolls attached to strings raise one hand and then another.

Telling us a Rajasthani tale as they dance with each other.

I dress up in a gota lehenga with a borla, bindi and bangles,
And dance the ghoomer to Rajasthani music as my nose ring dangles.

I wear a dark blue dhoti and a colourful mirrorwork vest.
And strum the ravanhatta, an instrument that sits on my chest.

e colourful turban and black moustache makes my papa look like a king
Mum looks beautiful in her leheria sari and shiny emerald ring.

Teevra misses his brothers and sisters so we drive to Ranthambore.
e green jeep takes us through the deep jungle and Teevra begins to roar.

Have you ever seen an entire city dressed up like a rainbow?

Holi is here and the Rajasthanis are soaked from head to toe.

All we see are pink girls and blue boys running through the town.

I try to hide but don't get far, I too look like a clown.

Jaipur has been an exciting adventure, we don't want to pack.

We will remember the magical stories and promise to come back.

1. Stationery items, Utensils, Hardware, Tin Trunks
2. Turbans, Tie and Dye Fabrics
3. Pickles and Sherbts
4. Jaipuri Quilts, Namkeens
5. Mojari, Handmade Crackers, Costume Jewellery
6. Semi-precious stones
7. Wholesale Market for Wedding Cards
8. Sarees
9. Sweets, Churans, Supari
10. Jewellery, Garments, Indian snacks
11. Precious & Semiprecious Stones
12. Lac Bangles, Jaipuri Quilts
13. Jewellery and Sarees
14. Marble Idols of various Gods
15. Lac Jewellery and Bangles
16. Jewellery and Kites
17. Rajasthani Print Textiles, local perfumes, Suparies & Churans, Camel skin shoes
18. Carpets
19. Pottery
20. Local musical Instruments
21. Mobile & Computer Accessories
22. Jewellery, Readymade Garments, Handicrafts, Books, Restaurants, Bangles
23. All things Rajasthani
24. Silver items
25. Sarees and Footwear
26. Electronics
27. Second Hand Vehicles
28. Handmade paper, Block Print Sarees, Furnishings
29. Vegetable Dye Block Print Sarees, Furnishings
30. Colourful Carpets

PALACE on WHEELS

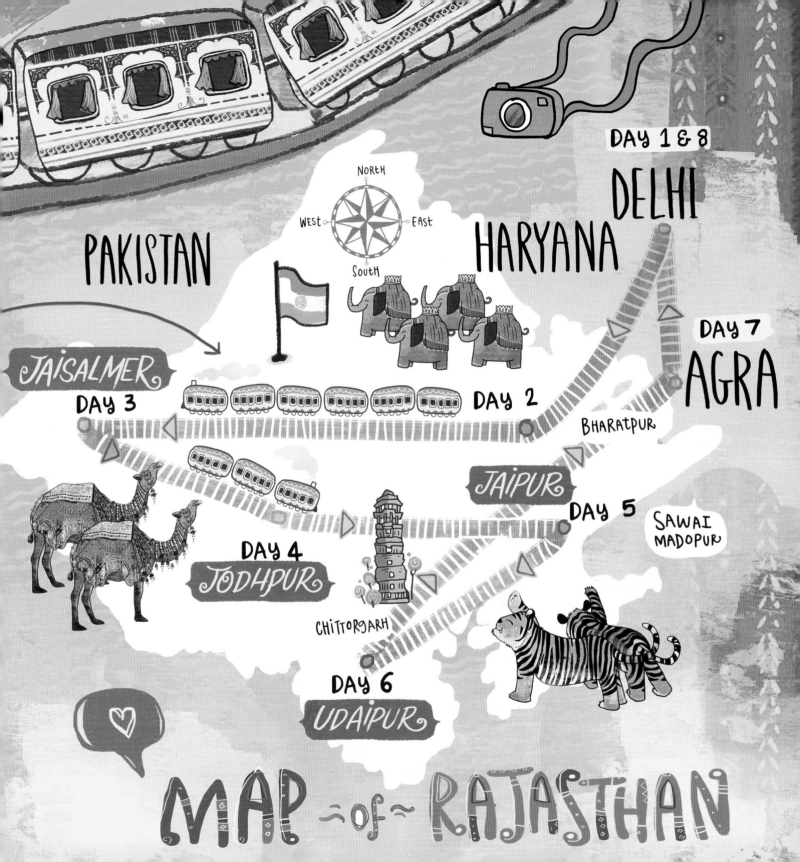

DAY 1 & 8

DELHI

HARYANA

PAKISTAN

NORTH

WEST — EAST

SOUTH

JAISALMER

DAY 3

DAY 2

DAY 7

AGRA

BHARATPUR

JAIPUR

DAY 5

SAWAI MADOPUR

DAY 4

JODHPUR

CHITTORGARH

DAY 6

UDAIPUR

MAP ~of~ RAJASTHAN

FACTS!

What colours are the cities of Rajasthan?

Jaipur is pink, Jodhpur is blue and Udaipur is white.

Which is the largest City in Rajasthan?

Jaipur

Why is Jaipur called the Pink City?

Jaipur was painted Pink as a sign of hospitality to welcome Prince Edward of Wales. It is one of the first planned cities of India.

Are there more people or animals on the streets in Jaipur?

There are more cows, camels and elephants than people on most streets in Jaipur.

Who is Jaipur named after?

Maharaja Jai Singh II, who ruled from Amer from 1699-1744 and Jaipur was founded in 1722.

Which is the most popular sport in Jaipur?

Polo

What are the most celebrated holidays in Jaipur?

Teej, Holi, Diwali, Gangaur, Kite Festival and Elephant Festival

What are some of the favorite foods that people in Jaipur like to eat?

Dal Bati Churma
Kachori
Ghevar

Which crafts are specially made in Jaipur?

Miniature painting
Marble and Sandstone carving
Kundan and Minakari Jewelry
Gemstone Cutting
Block printing